WHAT FOX KNEW

WHAT FOX KNEW

by Mary Barnes

AT BAY press

WINNIPEG

WHAT FOX KNEW

Design by Matthew Stevens and M. C. Joudrey.
Layout by Matthew Stevens and M. C. Joudrey.
Cover illustration by M. C. Joudrey.

Published by At Bay Press November 2019.

Library and Archives Canada cataloguing in publication is available upon request.

ISBN 978-1-988168-20-3 (print)
ISBN 978-1-988168-33-3 (e-book)

Printed and bound in Canada.

This book is printed on acid free paper that is 100% recycled ancient forest friendly (100% post-consumer recycled).

First Edition

10 9 8 7 6 5 4 3 2 1

atbaypress.com

In memory of Sarah and Alex, my parents

To Caitlin, Zach, Connor, and Cassie

Contents

Mary Barnes

Come to the River

The voice calls.
Come   sit on the flat rock
and watch as water glides over
these ancient stones.
Smells good eh? The air clean
the scent of pine gum piquant in the heat.
Listen. *Listen.* Hear that?
Beyond the calls
of crows and gulls
beyond the keening
cry of hawk
a drum beat
a dry chant
the Old Ones telling
you that you matter
that you are blessed.
Forget the day
on the school bus
when the boy with
the white teeth snapped
out *brown girl*
as if the words were
something dirty to be bleached
cleansed and rinsed.

But I sit here dreaming
snow falling past the window.
Birds flit in the juniper

for berries
and I discover I am
at the beginning of winter
the youthful summer
fading but not forgotten
while the town plow rumbles
                                        echoes
                                        along the floor

to my old and
slippered feet.

Long Time Ago

My father built a house of cured lumber
pounding nails into ceilings,
walls and floors. There we lived, my brothers,
our mother and I. On long winter nights
while wolves howled and
the arctic air cold-shouldered shorn trees
he warmed the place with a black and silver stove
that radiated heat into rooms
and into each of our souls.

My father tended a patchwork garden amidst
cedar, rough rocks and tall pine.
His murmurs in soft summer nights
                                        no match for the whippoorwill
spoke of chipmunks at the ripened strawberries
of raccoons in the crumbling compost

my mother's reply lost in the pillow
as September dreamed its way into fall.

My father sat on the cool veranda,
robins silenced by the noon sun,
rattler languid under the lilac.
He spun stories of cousins, uncles and aunts
gave us lessons that we be kind
that we be fair-minded to those we met.
The breeze beguiled
                                lingered and listened.

Now the house,
                    the land   and my father
sleep
while we recall the quick days we knew bliss.

Some Things Are Remembered

There was a summer
I heard the clang of a shovel
as my father
jostled the wheelbarrow
to the garden
to pull bindweed
that could choke the peas.

There was a summer
I heard flap of sheets
the sound crisp and white
as my mother
pinned them to the line.

There was a summer
my brothers brushed past me
riding invisible steeds
bound on an unknown quest to save
the world from danger.

Some things are remembered
the joy of a rainbow
the beauty of dew on morning grass
the flutter of wings in the maple
the snort of a deer
underneath the window.

What Fox Knew

Now shades remain
flitting
beneath the lilac
from the corner of my eye
on the path leading to the garden
reminding me
these are tokens of innocence
treasures to carry
through the days ahead
like the hand of the sun
on my back when there was a summer.

In That Place

Tree shaded the old house on the hill
nestled birds and squirrels in her branches
the little girl   the brothers seated
backs against her rough bark
telling stories
they knew Tree would keep secret.

In that place
Tree accepted the warm rain
spread her roots into the soil
stretched tall and waited
for the father to come home
        for the mother to call supper.

In that place
Tree guarded the sleeping family
as twilight settled on the flowing river
as Wind rustled leaves
shushed creatures large and small
as Moon rose above the pines and
smiled down in benevolence.

In the Yellow Afternoon

Her brothers climb piles of curing wood
their gleeful shouts
glancing off the woodshed walls
while she stands on wood chips
and wishes she were not in her
Sunday best   an ice blue dress
        her mother made
with work-worn fingers.
        The crushed cotton
bought from Anderson's Fabrics.

Itching to join her brothers
she thinks of the leaps she could make
to climb the highest
and beat them at their game.
She struggles with decorum
but her love of play, the high jinks
and their taunts   daring her
until
she steps
                    onto the first pile

snags and rips
a two-inch right-angled triangle in the perfect
                              circle of her skirt.

It will take some fine stitching to mend the hole.
She waits for the scolding
                                        to come
but her mother's mouth
is full of pins.

If You Stood on the Hill

you could see
the river run silver in the noonday sun
and to the southwest the high rock. Dark pine.
You could see Wind rush the poplars
clapping at her performance and aundaeg
                                                                 black-winged
call out his boisterous greeting.

At night under a fat moon you could
hear the train whistle in the distance
and wonder
            if one day you would go far.
When you went and discovered the new world
it was not what you dreamt of.   Was it?
Yet you did not forget the old river
nor the high rock
the day your sweet brother
fell into the dark water
and drowned
so small   so young
the day cool.
Spring new and
                inviting.

Expectations

Each spring she persuades her husband
to carry the galvanized tub outdoors
the same one
she once bathed their children in.
Taking turns, they scrubbed and splashed
until the water glowed milky with soap and dirt
while their laughter rang through the kitchen
the tub
            a boat for their voyage
the black and grey tiled floor their sea.
The vessel now ashore holds a lemon tree
the seed planted when the children grew up
and moved on.

Together she and he
lug the thing across the yard
and plonk it beneath the apple tree
dappled light playing on its rich glossy leaves.

Each summer while her husband works
she waits – a Penelope – watching
for the tree to bear flowers, for the vibrant
yellow fruit. She dreams of its scent, of
the taste mingling in drinks, cakes and pies.
But the tree remains silent and bare.

When her husband returns in the Fall
they drag the tub back to the house

back to the dark winter that lies ahead
to the place where they will think of
what they'd carried between them.

Girl in the Attic

Here I studied history
fought dates
sorted out wars
by the frosted glass.
A coat on my shoulders
I glanced at jars
queued on the windowsill
saw deer at windfall apples below
cars passing on the highway
unaware of the pleasures enjoyed
in this far and high country
that have come to pass:

Mother kneading bread with strong fingers
in the kitchen
brothers at play
while Father mends a tap
taking it apart.

Years pass and
as journey's end
draws near
one by one
they depart
. yet remain
forever in my heart.

The Road

The afternoon sun slows my steps
and I pause
at the end of the drive.
If I turn right I can walk down
the long sloping road to the highway
and stand by the mailbox
where the postman
brings news from the outside world.
If I go north I will come to the small village
where I can purchase bread and milk
                    a bag of chips. Orange Crush.
South takes me to town
all glitter and temptations
              hot roast beef sandwiches with gravy
Saturday night movies in a dimmed theatre.

If I turn left I can walk past
tall summer grasses and chicory's
blue heads nodding. The road brings me
to a canopy of trees where
small birds sleep
in the July heat. As my thin-soled sneakers
crunch on the dry lichened rocks
I begin dreaming
of fairies and elves
of bears down for their naps.
Or are they watching me
search for the elusive poem?

Perhaps it is caught in the nearby sprawling juniper
            an empty page waiting
for the words to descend, pure in the sunlight
a gesture of promise and enchantment
                                                  yet to come.

Too Far Ahead

Evening and dusk settles
on the dusty road
bathed in shadow where my mother,
my children and I walk. I'm walking quickly
when my daughter calls out
Mom! Wait. You're too far ahead.
I turn and see what I have missed,
the children jostling,
laughter ringing in the air.

We pass ferns
their brown-tipped fronds
extending to the earth,
full-headed milkweed and bees
in masses gathering nectar,
the scent of blooms
pungent in the blushing twilight.

My mother leans forward
on her walking stick,
smiles with contentment and
I see
the wisdom of the child.

Inheritance

She is leafing through
the albums of her mind
sorting and discarding   trying
to paste the relations she wants
to the story she intends to present
but images appear angled
and out of reach. Like dervishes
they spin and spin
until they lie lifeless
                                    jangled.

The ancestors came, my mother says,
out of countries beggared by war
                              depleted by famine
                              shackled by religious censure.
Sailing on the first tide of hope
they slipped from chains
                                         cold and binding
to step on shores less errant. They rose
through the strength of their backs to create
new generations who spread
across the land like a raiment.

They lived and loved this way, a proud race
toiling, begetting, and spending for our benefit.
Then one day we, their descendants, forgot
who they were   sepia photographs
                    confined to attics and we the progeny

brushed aside beginnings.

The Old Ones went on –
why do we not realize thunder without lightning
is not a storm; that the seed and the root
are needed for the building of a tree?
Else
we are without shape
                    ghostly
tattered relics seeking solidity.

My mother's hand in mine is real.

The Dream

They came as she lay asleep
as great welts of white
blew down the street
driven by a northerly
beating at the window
                                        covering the pavement.
They rose in the darkened room
flickering images of people long past.
She wanted to ask why
they hovered – were they real or shade?
There was a woman in a red dress
bending to a flower
a man at a blue gate turned and smiled…
she did not recognize any of them
but they felt familiar
characters from a well-beloved book.
She wanted to turn the next page
but she woke of a sudden
                                             the dream gone.
A dog in the neighbourhood howled.
When she stirred
to start the new day
breaking the veil
between here and there
she could have wept
for the happiness captured
                                             in that one moment
then lost

a line drawn
a step not taken
as morning grew and the
sun brushed
at the fringe of the sleeping suburb.

Brown

Hey brown skin. Get outta the way.
you bawl from the car
horn honking
then speed down the highway
as if you have some place important to go.
Browned-off
I watch the dust settle behind you then
think   yeah
brown is the mixture – no – balance of red
                                        yellow and black
rich as Mother Earth on a summer's day
when Wind blows against her
subtle as deer
appearing in the woods
with delicate steps to nod and wish you well
steadfast as grizzly   Kitchi-Mukwoh – spirit bear
who guards us in our travels   who heals
savoury as the pudding Grandmother makes
with apples, raisins and brown sugar
served with tea from
the round-bellied Brown Betty.
I am in a brown study
about the word you malign
                                        abuse and belittle.

Brown is a good colour.
                                Heh!

not on the agenda

this land most times in the summer is dusty the wind blowing through the long grasses by the baseball field the winter can be cold to the bone our people were meant to be hunters you wronged our people placing us on this land you call a reservation we have lived here all these years like children banished to a closet we do not even treat our children this way today my sister works in whitebread jobs to put food on the table and last month my auntie jane vanished when she went to the store to buy milk the stone-faced cops ignored our pleas and said we were not on the agenda just like those guvment shirts up in parliament later we found her blood on the snow outside town and I wondered how long will our people have to bleed

Kevin 1

I used to tell your cousin, Kevin,
to be more tolerant.
Be aware of what you're doing, I'd scold.
Well. He said, did I know
that his old man
beat the crap out of his mother every chance he got
filled to the gills 'cause he can't hold a job,
shamed by the white man's words,
you're nothing but an Indian anyway
nothing but a savage.

He'd go on, they cut my grandfather's hair
hitched him to a plow when all he knew was hunting.
My grandmother found him one morning
choking on his blood, insides poisoned
by the hooch he got from a bootlegger
down on sherbourne.

His mother told him these stories
out of sight of the man who was his father
before the blows from his fists came and slammed her
into next week.
And you want me to be more *tolerant*, he'd yell.
Don't beat on the kids at school.
Well, what the hell do you know, Aunty?

Kevin 2

You want to know more about Kevin.
Last time, well, he was hurting eh?
All that anger?
I told him:
See that sun?
That's Geeziss.   Father Sun.
Kevin said his father died
                    on the streets
long time ago
from alcohol poisoning
            just like his grandfather.

I said
    Father Sun is the flame
that never dies.
Clouds or night may cover his face
but he is always there
a beautiful spirit who will shine
down the days.
Kevin said not a word and went away.

Next time I saw him shaking his fist
                        at Father Sun.
By and by I saw Kevin again.
This time
        he raised his arms wide.
Father Sun sat in the sky
and shone and shone and shone.

Territory

My sister, your Aunt Emmy, told me this story:

We are inside the lines, a 90-foot square
where we've always played since the ghost people came.
You're a utility player
your hand a mitt
meant to catch the heaters the fouls
and cradle my love.

I'm a pitcher and from the hill
I've played backdoor sliders
Closers even nail downs
to keep our loving safe – this I didn't see coming.

You do
a punchout
slam your leathered fist into the
slender ridge of my jaw.
You slug the soft flesh of my chest
and bat the delicate orb of my eye.
When you look
into my blackened eye and swollen face
you know you have struck out.

I'm no Baseball Annie
with simpering smiles and soft hands.
I want to drive a worm killer down the field.
Stumbling

What Fox Knew

I follow the narrow beam of light
shining on the wall
and walk to the front foyer.
I lay down the glove
pick up the bat
weigh it and think of what I could do:
drive a dinger   a tape-measure   a tater over
the fence
and run the bases full-tilt.

But with Ruthian power
I steel myself
and think
beyond the diamond
to the next sun rise
the next bird song
the embrace of my Elders.
I hear a drumbeat
a voice
telling me to be aware of the good life.

I lay down the bat
And say through bruised lips:
Time out. We need to talk.

She's some talker, that Aunty of yours.

Nottawasaga Bay Morning

You park the car
and stride towards the beach
where grey-wool clouds ride low
over the bay   on a wind
that curls water onto shore.

Seven geese line the sand
the lead walks into the surf
and with tentative steps
the others follow then float
on the white caps before taking off
straight as an arrow
flying.
            Circling.

And your heart lifts
joyous, its beat as loud as the waves
pounding in your ears.
You understand then
you are a part of
the Great Mystery
the Creator
Kitchi-Manitou.

The Ancestors are Speaking

Impatient for the road,
you drum your fingers on the windshield,
aching to be anywhere but here.
I cross the field,
dew darkening the red of my skirt
while grasses sway
at Wind's bidding.
Heavy-headed Joe Pye weed
Oswego tea and the chicory nod.
I stop to hear their whispers
Remember us. Remember
our ways and follow them.
I look towards the car and call out:
Listen. The ancestors are speaking.
Your head bowed
busy at the car radio
searching for that elusive song
that will take you from our world
and I despair.
Then you look up
come to join me
and I know you have heard.

Regeneration

Daughter, I am the Woman murdered.
I am the Woman dragged from the
mean streets, from sunlit parks and
the waterfronts.
I am the one they took into the woods
and flung in the cold, unrelenting water.

Though they think they have won,
I will rise and find my way back
reclaim the woods, the streets and parks –
my place.

Tell the stars I am coming.
Tell the moon to light my way.

Nightfall

Sleep eludes me and I think of the
violets you picked the spring we met.
They haunt me
your smile shy
at my acceptance
and all last summer
our hands stayed clasped
with a promise to our future.

The quarrel came of a sudden
like a cruel November wind.
You wanted me to step into your world
                deny my people.
When I refused you hurled words – stones
that bruised:

squaw, brown girl, no account.

We continued to argue, each word lost
in the shadowy wood,
then you struck. Punched. Kicked.
And the only thing I could see
besides your foul fists
was a dried leaf trembling in the oak above.

Battered
            I rose and fled
turning once to glimpse

the mauve jacket I'd worn
lying crumpled in the snow
where you'd thrown it
after you pulled at the hood
a sleeve   outstretched
as if seeking help.

I have walked the path since
in daylight and at nightfall
the jacket
hanging from a cedar branch
where I placed it
a flag, a representation
that I am conversant with the lost,
that I am mindful of the missing.

It is we who seek justice.
It is we who want worth.

Woman Missing

Wait — wait.
Okay, let's construct the scene again.
Maybe she was walking down the street near the river
and maybe under an indigo moon. Don't laugh.
Now it could be there was a wind. Or rain.
Maybe the weather was good, the sun shining.
I suppose we'll never know. Let's not dwell on that.
Say she wanted to rekindle an old friendship.
Say they met at the bridge
in a place open and fair
not the dark wood everyone thinks of.
Gather the evidence. Remember it.

Hell. How do we find her in all this snow?

Blue Sky Woman

I am drunk today
pie-eyed on Blue Sky
her skirt billowing wide
while the breeze chatters at leaves
and the sun rolls bright upon the world.
On the beach, the sand sparkles, and out on the water
waves jostle for shore,
                                        come only when invited
teased by an incoming wind.

Can you hear that sound?
Beyond the susurrus of the
waves? A voice calling softly.
Is it from some distant shore,
a place we know nothing of?
What word does it bring?
What news?

What do you offer? Another bright day.
Sky flashing so blue she
burns the eyes? And in the silence
of noon, I listen, ears attuned, and hear
birds rustling in their nests,
the distant barking of a dog,
the gurgle of neighbour's pond
like a river in spring, full of hope.
The whispers of plants telling bees:
Hurry. Hurry.

These days will soon end.

Quietly, quietly,
mushrooms in the grass
tilt their oversized brown caps
to Blue and her intoxicating smile.

What Fox Knew 1

What Fox knew
was that the people
living at the house were temporary.
Their boxes crowded room after room.
There was no unpacking.
At noon he watched from the hill
as they hauled in wood for the cold nights ahead.
Each evening a fire burned brightly
smoke climbing the night sky.
Then one crisp morning,
the sun pink and rising from its bed
                                        they left.
Where Fox could not say. Perhaps
they crossed the river.
They left the house chilled and lonely.
They left him
a scrap of hard crust thrown
carelessly on the snow.

It would not last the day.

What Wind Knew

What Wind knew
was that the man
struggling to plant seed
in the glade beyond the forest
was too old to bend.
Under the late morning sun
he poked his cane
into the soil
                    dropped in the seeds
and tamped them with his scuff-toed boot.
Wind knew of the long wait
knew the seed would grow
watered by rains and warmed by the sun.

She knew long after the man was gone
the land would remember
that the time would come
for her to approach Fox
standing on the hill
and ruffle his fur.
She knew too Fox would lift
his snout and sniff the air
before trotting towards the river
where there were many stories to tell.

What Fox Knew 2

What Fox knew
was that after the people had left
deer picked their way
over the sleeping garden.
Nosed the abandoned birdfeeder
and peered in the frosted window.
Wary of his presence
a pair of hares
                    ears twitching
leaped forward and sniffed the
tracks left by the lodgers.
When the moon rose
over the snowscape
a lone timber wolf
climbed the rocky crag
and howled his song
to the ice-bound river.
Fox saw the house
longing
for warmth
shift and shudder.

What River Knew

What River knew
was that the star, falling,
would settle on the water
and drift towards the reeds.
Wind had whispered this news the day before.
Turtle crept to the edge of the bank
and raised her head
in welcome.
When the stars appeared
to bless the silken sky,
River heard Frog
sing from the marsh his song.
When the sun streaked the sky pink,
River heard a rustle
saw Swan unfold its wings,
                                        embrace the star
                                        heard the feathery voice
of the water lily say

                                                Home.

The Hunt

Fox knew it was not important
that he hunt the hare
                                        catch it and
carry it up the rise.
Fox knew it was not vital
that he climb the rocky land near the river
deliver
            and place it at the door of the den.
No. Winter had come.
Snow now blocked the trails
and the growing burn in his chest
made movement slow.
His frame was thin.
His coat had the wear and tear of a faded leaf.
The scope of his terrain narrowed
the fire of hunting gone.
He remembered springs past,
his returns to the bottomland
peppered with new growth
where he once found moles. Mice
in the warm sun.
But the pull of that dream
the constant ache in his heart
and he knew that the
Old Ones were near,
perhaps in those cedars.
He thought he heard his name
                                                            Waugoosh.

Perhaps it was time to pare down,
to relinquish the stars.
Perhaps it was time to talk to Wind.

Magic

What the man saw
as he stepped from the birch grove
was the hummingbird
hovering
            the heft and whir of its slight wings
the fox at the edge of the meadow
the morning breeze like a cat's paw
tapping the daisies
a glamour he could not explain.
Frowning,
            he saw the fox stoop
and drink at the river's bank
water dripping from its chin.
Then he sensed that he and the fox
the flowers
                  the birds
were all strummers
                        who give flesh to the day
flooding it with colour,
with hope.
                  With joy.

In Bleak Mid-Winter

From the window I watched the charging wind
ride the snow across lawns
leap the fence and swirl
around chairs left at summer's quick retreat.
I watched it trot up porch steps to the door and
on the way startle roses slumbering.

I thought of you, my battle-weary
soldier, trapped in a frail February twilight
in a land amid graves
swirls of sand, wind
and sun, called to a bleak war by old men,
sleek men with their hot and insistent words.

I imagined you ghost-eyed
                    heart aching
for home. I imagined you coming to walk
in our forest, snowshoes crunching
beneath your feet. The snap of frost-filled woods.
I imagined my hot fingers blossoming
spring on your sunburnt and scarred skin
                              melting a love
grown bitter and cold on the last parting.

With a flick of its tail the wind moves on
leaving a blanket of white on dead lawns,
on a heart longing for spring.   You.

April

The pansies are less cheerful this morning
their velvet faces buried in snow from
a cock-eyed storm that fell in the night,
spring delayed by winter's cold hand.
Too long the trees have stood and shivered bare
limbs crackling   snapping
under the arctic wind.
Too long I have waited at the window
numbed by your departure.
What did we quarrel about?
Some meaningless thing
like the placement of a fork or a spoon
then an unkind word on a slippery tongue
that twisted love out of shape.
Where did you go
leaving our warm bed for the cold?

A dark figure walks up the drive
hunched inside a down-filled coat and my heart leaps.
But it is only the man come to read the gas meter.
I thought it was you.

Returning.

Now I long for your smile, to heal our differences
the way the sun melts frost on the grey-bearded trees
that line the silent streets of our town.
Here comes April at last   yawning

dressed too lightly
for the bleak landscape
                    bringing sunlight.
Can May be far behind?

Fair Wind

The day we sailed
out on the bay
sky cerulean blue
cirrus clouds
water glistening
you turned and smiled.
I meant to tell you
I loved you
but then the wind died
and we sat
motionless.

I moved to start
the five-horsepower
press dead ahead for shore.
You shook your head and
said, *let's wait*
for a wind
to rise.

The Comforter

Nothing is sturdy
these days. Was a time
you could buy something – anything –
and it would last.

Look at this comforter – I bought it for
the colour. Lemon yellow. Cost a pretty penny too.
Two years old and it needs mending. And
didn't I have a time
finding a patch to match the fabric.

Look at these hands – they're my mother's –
brown, creped with blue veins
like the ones that kneaded bread
                                        washed clothes
wiped noses and
guided you towards womanhood.
Look girl, your fingers are shaking.

It's the Little Things

I'm in the kitchen with my silver
about to remove the black from your Aunty Laura's
                                        butter knife
the pale morning sun seeking entrance at the patio door
as I remember days I flitted along narrow lanes
from school to her cool curtain-drawn house
where I ate bologna sandwiches
while she pressed me for news from home.

Now look, my son, here's the baby spoon I used
to provide the nourishment you needed.
My, how you changed some from
plump infant to boy and it seems
rushed towards manhood.

And here is the long-handled pickle fork
I used to plunge down vinegary pools
for that last white and elusive onion.
It's the little things   each detail buffed
with fondness that
kindles the memory and
                              polishes the heart.

See

Grey fog
obscures
the headland
now slate blue
not bottle green
grey clouds
hang low
unseen wind
pushes
grey water
to the shore.

Gulls on the
sand
huddle
          confer
about
the canoeist
gliding on the
pewter surface
of the bay.

Grey fog
obscures
the headland
now slate blue
not bottle green
grey clouds

hang low
unseen wind
pushes
grey water
to the shore.

Gathering

Nip of frost
woodsmoke apples
windfalls on the grass
Russian sage on fingers
bee balm leaves
later for tea.

Inhale clouds
shadowing the sky
blush of sun.

Breathe night coming on.

The Hat

I went up the sloping rock
to the opened red
gate and there you were. Pulling weeds.
Our eyes met and not a word was said but
a lock of your hair fell when you pushed back
your dark and stained felt garden hat. The one you took
from the wooden rack, placing it on your
head
with a firm pat before you went out the door. Each
day you carried out the act. As if it was a prayer
of hope,
to bless the seeds, to give each plant its due.
Then all things in hand, day done,
you returned from the land and
hung the hat on its peg.

Lighthouse

Backward and forward, waves frantic at his feet.
His heart too, thinking of Margaret so near death
in the cottage behind him, dark curtains drawn.

Only forty and she's got cancer
eating at the beauty of her.
And he unfamiliar with the land of sickness.

He looks across the bay and peers through the
fog and rain
sees a shadowy structure. He is searching
for what he does not know. He's exhausted.
His heart flooded. Sinking.
                    His anchor lost.
A wind comes up and pushes aside the fog.
Tendrils drift and he sees the lighthouse clearly now
the crumbling white tower luminescent
          on the distant shore.

She has shone through
all the storms year after year
leading him safely home.
He gulps back a sob
turns and hurries
towards the land. He hopes
he's not too late.

We Talk

All Saints' Day and my knife thrusts deep
into Jack's head while you tell me
your heart is dying.
I go past the thick skin, dig through to guts,
separating seed and tendril and pulp.
We talk, you telling me
of wealds, downs and mews in
your place of birth,
your eyes shining in remembrance.

We talk of books,
Dumont's latest, *The Pemmican Eaters,* her adoration for Gabriel
words dancing before my eyes
buffalo runner, coulees, cranberry and fireweed.
You spin your favourites,
stories of the theatre, of
Lee, Olivier, and Dench.

Tears swell and
leaves flying their last flight
blur
as they pass by the window.

The knife slips and
as I watch my life's force
seep from my finger

soak the grabbed towel
I think of your heart beating slower. And slower.
The doorbell rings: it's the neighbour
leaving daffodil bulbs to plant.
We continue slicing pulp into chunks
placing them in water to stew
dreaming of pies and muffins we can make
this winter.
You smile
take my hand and say you
will plant the daffodil bulbs.

When you are asleep
I walk the lovely woods
listen to the roar of the wind
in the birches and pines
thinking of the times we had
                    the times we will have.
Later I will pick
                    up the pieces and throw
them into the compost
feeding the mole I know lives beneath the bin.
I know I too
                    must prepare for my next meal.

Honey, I Cried

Rain dripping
from the roof,
echoes of Eliot's month
as I gaze out the
attic window at the
honey-gold lumber
piled below
turned to dark amber.
In November's graveyard grey evening,
Emmylou Harris moans
of heartache and make-believe.

How long has it been—a day, week, a month
since the headlights of your Chevy truck
edged into the driveway
and you stepped from the cab
to swipe your John Deere hat
across your knee,
looked up at the house
to see me standing there.

But wait, this poem isn't about you.

Red Balloon

It was not the kumquats
cradled in my hands
glowing orange and
ready for preserves.

It was not the barrel of grapes
ripe and plump for wine-making
or the click of the raven's tongue
as he perched above in the oak
that had me stop and wonder on the why of things.

I thought it a mirage
but as it floated shimmering above me
I came to see it was
a gift of love.

For all the nickels there are in the world,
for all the words there are in the dictionary,
I hold this to be true.
There is no time to waste.
The thing to do is scramble up the slope of the sky
to reach for the red balloon hovering there
Do not be shunted aside by roiling
clouds   or the mocking wind.
Do not let the tirades of humans
grate upon your ears
and stop you from your endeavours.

Mary Barnes

Be direct in your perceptions
and as credit follows hope
be as bold as the river rolling to the sea.

The Game

I think we should get married
she said, dreaming of domesticity,
babies and a ring. *Hold on* he said,

                                        wanting to run.
Will he miss drinks with his buddies
and drives down country roads, the
wind rushing, tearing at his youth?

Sixty years later
his steps slow and faltering
his mind full of holes
he says
You forgot the butter.
No. She points to the dish on table
then touching his shoulder
she murmurs
Tag. You're it.

Along the Wooded Path

Along the wooded path twilight filters
through the forest green
on leaves layered
like pages in a book
each one waiting to be
discovered and perused.
And around each gentle bend
they walk, she two steps ahead
yet close enough that should he stumble
she could catch his fragile bulk
                                        curved to a C with age.
She stops. His halting steps soon join hers,
a Monarch alighting on his shoulder.
Leaves flutter. Together they emerge to stand in the sun.

Friday Evening (for Audrey)

There's a party on the beach
to celebrate a birthday,
a special year ending in a zero,
hearts swelling to think of such a moment.

Inside the great room the piano tinkles,
someone is playing 'I Dreamed a Dream'
and the music spills into the soft evening air,
sails over the smoke-grey waters lapping at the shore.
The sound moves out across the bay
                                        joins the sun
splashing notes on the painted sky.

In the twilight people gather
in gentle circles of conversation
where some whisper   some laugh
while some speak a last word
before the sun sets
the stories important as the day that
is passing.
Joy is in the air: she reaches down
                                                    touches each heart.

Chords

Strum the strings and evoke the
green days of summer:
the carefree laughter of delight
at a frog discovered
its quivering skin smooth and wet
an ant assuming the load
of his civilization
and not a whimper from him.
There comes the song of a mother
knee-deep in ferns
searching for wild strawberries
sun-kissed and
succulent
perfect for jamming.

Another chord and
autumn falls:
brown, burnished and golden.
The seasons are fleeting.
Hasten now and praise trees
wind-swept and bare,
migrating geese wings
bent against a November sky.

Enter Winter
that white-haired conductor
setting his own tune.
Deer gather to listen

then take the message
to people like me
who are waiting.
Cheeby-aub-oozoo, the musician, comes and
gathers all the music.
We match his step
to the drum that he beats and
march into a new country
pristine and still,
to a new tune
of a promising new spring.

Upset

The sudden snow
on this April morn
has the daffodils shivering
and the birds
wandering
the white sky
seeking warmth.
The crow in his black frock
strutting the lawn
seems to have forgotten
what he wanted to say.
Then a single word erupts:
Repeated.   Aborted.
A strangled cry:
                              Aw.
Aw – aw.

Testament

With trust and a scuffed trowel
she kneels,
cuts a furrow two feet long
then another, six inches away
dropping in store-bought seeds
hoping   praying they will
                                grow.
Pressing them into
the earth
she gently covers them and
tamps the soil.
She takes the
watering can   sprays the earth.

Over the span of summer
heart-shaped leaves
climb and curl
around the metal trellis,
bloom blue flowers,
morning glories
the size of saucers
while bumblebees travel into
their hearts for nectar then
emerge drunk on pollen
their plump bodies
                        glowing in the sun.

Persistent, she plants year after year

seeking insight into the deaths of her
brother, her father. Her mother.

Time insinuates its constraints.
What is life?
A beginning. A kernel.
A heart to be nurtured.

Country Food

It is the first day
of harvest
and I pull a carrot from the soil

wipe it clean

on my printed cotton dress
chomp on country air
taste September sunshine and
the sweetness of Mother Earth.

On An April Morning

Listen. I ask you.
What is it we seek:
the garish lights
of a broad billboard
or the cinematic view
in a darkened theatre
or sailboats plying warm waters?
Is it in the anemic iceman
seeking refuge
from the mild
April winds?
Is it the creatures
skirting the hidden coves
and inlets on that far shore?
Yes. And more.

It is in the windswept beach
Emmylou on the radio
singing *tender ladies*
rain drumming on the car roof,
beads and ripples coursing the windshield,
gulls challenging the iron-grey sky
for shining days ahead,
for the return of the plovers.
All that gives me pause like the
suddenness of thunder.

Look at the low-hanging clouds

enshrouding the sand-filled and melting floes
that feel primordial.

If we enlist our eyes our ears
our hearts
our imagination can say:

this is
spring.

Stain

She weaves a trail
through the dense
undergrowth amid
yellowed ferns
tufts of grass not green
and comes upon three large cans
of paint   previously unseen
by walkers passing
through the wood.

Were it not for their shape
              so odd   so round

Were it not for how raggedly
they stood   broken soldiers
bleeding white
upon the damp ground
she too would have
walked on.
She picks them up
sets them beside the trail
and hopes
next spring's growth can reseed,
hopes too
that she has not failed.

Windstorm

How we strive
following the tradition of our ancestors
pushing, pushing the earth into hills
to create labyrinthine tunnels
that will suit our need.
Once we saw the tip
of the moon.
Were we toiling that long?

Then a sudden windstorm
sweeps away our work
and helpless we watch
as it whirls
off to Africa
or perhaps Australia with our homes.

But soon silence reigns. No more wind.
The air haunted with the aftermath of dust
and the knowledge
we must start again.
Digging
          saving what is not destroyed.
We'll build new houses and rooms
large enough for storage and new families.
Yes, we will build anew and forgive
the woman with her broom.

Reflection

My cousin lifts his oar
water glinting silver
points to the white and gold
of water lilies.

Painted in my mind:
the canoe, oars, sunlight
and the dark-haired kinsman
expounding beauty.

Our journey that day—
sailors on the open depths—
translucent once but now
blurred to the thick skin of time.

Tracking the Mystery

It had been a quiet night,
the wind dying after the day's storm.
A night of deep black   Creator's mystery
a time of spirits
and yet, try as I might
I could not find meaning.

The delicate dawn
brought light softly to the snow
and I saw them more clearly.
Deer tracks they were.
Circles. Figure eights and trails.
The animals had milled around the yard.
Then silent. Still. Waiting.

What purpose was theirs
to gather there?
Did they come with a message?
Leaving the window,
I went about the tasks of the day
wondering if I was following
the true way.

Night after night, the deer returned,
and in the morning, more tracks appeared,
their nimble hooves creating a design
before the bare-limbed oak
crystallized by frost and cold

infinity
timelessness
written there

The Cherry Tree

I am surrounded by trees, young and old,
a forest of friends amid fern and
flower, yet I seek your company
to walk unencumbered on the path
to pass from this shaded weald
through weather intemperate and sublime
to defy any opposition or wrath
and go into the sun, into the open fields.

What you must see, what you must bridge
and along the way gather, blooms over time.
But I am merely a tree, dear poet,
rooted to this ground--
oh, soon to be cut down on this wintry ridge.

The sawyer saw me leaning so dealt the blow
and now here I lie, rusted blood upon the snow.

Afternoon Tea

There are
clothes to launder,
floors to sweep, and meals to make
but I am distracted.
Stepping from beneath the oak
I attend to flowers,
deadheading petunias,
marvelling at bees
in foxgloves,
at a hummingbird playful in the cedar.

Dance

I walk upon the beaten path.
It's neither day nor night
but the hour of between
when fairies flit and roam
the shadowy wood.
A deer appears,
her tawny skin glowing
in the half-light.
We observe each other, and then I say *Hello*.
She bows her head, steps onto the trail
and I speak once more,
my words gentle and hushed.
She takes two steps forward, lifts her legs high
as in a dance, and so do I.
The breeze in the trees sings
its sweet refrain.
Lowering her head,
she bows and
I follow suit. When I look up
she is gone. Has disappeared.
Was she ever there?

The Pulse of the Garden

I wonder about the garden.
Will I be able to dig
in the days to come,
to pull weeds beginning to sprout,
scrape away the mess from winter?
The days grow shorter and my own life force,
once vibrant,
seems to have gone on a journey to
a different place.
If I hesitate in my shovelling
to see a bean grow
a pansy bloom
or a tomato gleam red
in the September sun,
will my heart, weary, skip its beat,
and slow my pace for the days ahead?

For now, I shall be bold and
feel the wind
full of expectation on my face.
For now, I shall bend my ear
to the gentle whispers of the cedar tree
and dance to the steady rhythm
of the earth beneath my feet.

In the Old Graveyard

What life did you have
before they laid you
beneath these grey stones
beside this old church,
amid dry grasses blowing
on this brown hill?

Perhaps, you were a
farmer, housewife,
maiden—
                child.

Maybe you tilled,
baked, yearned for love.
Played.

Did you fall
beneath the plow,
go mad in the wilderness,
die of a broken heart,
succumb to a cough?

Who wept and
why?
Were kind words said?

A hymn?
A prayer?

Who wept and
why?
Who misses you now?

The Cut

Why he left, she doesn't know.
Where did he go? To the ancients, she wonders?
Standing at the window, she recalls
that once upon a misty morn,
he raised his scythe and sliced
the air alive, splinters of hay
anointing him in golden rain.

Was it that cut at the sky
that sent him falling
                                        her world falling
and split their world in two?

Why he left, she doesn't know
and the redbird whistling in the tree,
his notes as sharp and definite as the blue sky,
even he
        is of no help.

Mary Barnes

Remembering Ottawa, October 22, 2014

Waiting for spring
you watch squirrels criss-cross the snow-filled yard
as if they are playing tic-tac-toe.
You see the cobalt blue of a bold jay
swoop for seeds,
the cardinal's fleeting blush,
a January sun dancing
soft beams of light
                    long-fingered
upon the wide planked floor.
You think about grandparents long gone
and wonder if they sent these good spirits,
these precious blessings to lessen the blow
of exploding guns on that far-off hill,
news that shot through every heart in the
villages and towns of this dear country.

Widow

Wrapped in his red and black mackinaw
she stands on the shore
and reflects on her man now gone,
on the shared laughter,
the quarrels that sparked
and sometimes caught fire,
the stillness of nights
wrapped so tight
there seemed but one beating heart
before death
silenced his.

She has reached a valley,
a watershed.
Which way to turn?

The wind hollers down the bay,
wakes her from this
wasteland of grief
to declare of things to come.
A storm to clean the air.
Grey clouds gather, ride in,
folding and unfolding
until they darken the sky.
Gusts churn the sand from its bed.
The thick water glitters green,
swells, crests, foams white.

She lifts her chin
opens her coat
as rain begins to fall
the wind catching her hair,
teasing the blue-striped dress
she wore to the funeral,
briskly scrubbing her face of tears
the way her mother did years ago
with the edge of her printed apron.

And over the rush of the wind
she hears the words:
I know it hurts but it's
time to move on.

Nottawasaga Notes

Thursday,
3 days before Hallowe'en,
and after a dental checkup,
I steer the car down Main Street
over the blue bridge
through pouring rain and a driving wind,
the wipers smacking in frenzy.
At Old Mosley
I glimpse the water,
the beach remains hidden by
stores. Boarded up now
                                        that summer's gone.
The radio is playing the Raider's March
and I want to drive faster,
have an adventure of my own.
Several puddles later
I stop at the post office. The women at the counter
are giggling with a customer
about something burnt — I hear only
a partial conversation. I pay for my parcel
return to the car and continue
across town. Around a bend
a gusting wind herds fallen leaves
across the street.
At the box store I rush inside,
weave my cart among customers,
a bearded man in jeans and a striped navy shirt
buying a bouquet of carnations,

past a diminutive white-haired woman smiling.
At the produce counter I survey packaged strawberries,
mangoes and apples
before selecting a dark green broccoli tree, a yellow
pepper
then down to the bread aisle where I
choose a loaf of potato and chive focaccia.
What is this poem about?
An image appears
of cooking lunch for my mother and she says,
It's good to see you.
I want to cry — it's been
a year since she
crossed the river.

Let Us Sleep

You dredge up the poor souls every chance
you get when you begin your bloody wars
as if we are the force for your vile dance.

Let me say this before you go too far:

us blokes didn't know about the war then.
Signed up for adventure, young blood boiling
for a chance to get away from routine
pushing manure, cutting lumber. Toiling.

We never had a chance. Rain fell. Mates too.
Guns shattering the grey skies and green plain,
blood flowering in mud-filled trenches so
nothing grew over those who were slain.

Now every November there are parades,
flags flown to honour those who served. Who fell.
I say, let us sleep. Stop your mean charade.
Let us poor buggers sleep. Us now. Did well.

The Awakening

The day after the ice storm
I go for a walk
treading the trail
                my steps careful
mindful of
any hidden ice
                         my head bowed
when I sense a presence.

I glance up and see a deer,
its face turned towards me.
She takes a step forward.
I do not move
and in the stillness
the only sound I hear
is the steady
                   dripping from the trees.

How alive the air is,
winter bathing us in its alabaster light.
But I am a beggar here,
wanting answers
wondering what awakening this is.

My heart throbs
                          the fragile moment not to be broken.

Out of the past a memory:

What Fox Knew

I see your young face,
hear the laughter you brought with your teasing.
We knew such felicity.
The need to understand
lies like a deep
dark river
between us
the same one that held you fast
in its cursed current
then in a blink of an eye
wrenched you away.

There was no warmth that day
despite the sun,
despite the mellifluous notes of songbirds
in the murmuring pines.

Later, while the fox
stood shyly at the garden's border,
I heard the far-off whistle of the train
headed south for the city
but my mind was on you that day:
What could erase such sorrow?
How to find the path beyond
this river of discontent?

Yet the river is not to blame.
And here you are, my brother, I whisper.

The deer flicks its ears once
then vanishes
                    down the trail
into the deep and
                   dark forest.

What a Collection

I don't know what the ravens are saying this
morning of green tenderness and
rain but, my, what a collection of
squallings and cracklings and whistles…
– Mary Oliver, "Ravens"

The sky is sharp
as a
blue pencil
while the March sun
trundling north meets ice.
Chickadees flit at feeders,
fly over
sleeping gardens hidden beneath the white canvas of
snow.

I sit at the window and wonder
on the grandeur of things,
how little I know, how
I don't know what the ravens are saying this
day in their black chuckling
as they wing over frosted rooftops
dipping into tall jack pines and bare oak.

What could they be saying?
What message lies inside their clever
cawing?
Do they speak of walks upon the sand,

of days ahead soft as lilac,
or is the spouting a show, a persuasion
this grand *morning of green tenderness and rain*
and affectionate winds? I think
the sooty-caped jackdaws,
mischief makers, are teasing me with
their rowdy remarks,
beating out with measured stridency
the news that
Spring sends her love,
but has decided to wait until
Winter
                    dragging his heels
departs. *But my, what a collection of*
snares, bamboozling me with their ranting.
Long-legged on jack pines they
mock me in my fever
to walk barefoot
on the verdant green.

Why not write a Dear John letter
or talk to Fox? I would have to
wait as long for that
favoured season to appear.
Still they minister to my heart with their

squallings and cracklings and whistles…

Train's Coming Through

Pages ripped open, words taking flight;
behold them pitch Tolstoy's first-rate work.
Train's coming through the dark winter night.

Gowns fall away, the glittering rooms,
there too falls Vronsky, Anna and son.
Scandal rocks Moscow, husband finds out.
Where's the page he shows hate, shows scorn?
Why toss out Tolstoy?
Why throw the classic into the bin?
There goes Kitty, Levin, happy and bright,
the landscape of Russia, the simple life.
Pages slide from fingers, careless and light.
Vronsky's left, Anna's on the run.
Train's coming through the dark winter night.

Barry's Song (for Barry Dempster)

Barry scores each white space
with songs of boots, God, the stars,
horses and desire.

Words burst off the page:

up they ride into the night sky
and there hang like lanterns
in our dark.

That Which Is and That Which Strives to Be

The bear in my dream
blocks every door of
the mall from which I try to leave
except one.

He presses me to follow
a narrow and well-worn path
where Van Gogh's flowers, either side of me,
lean over a fence,
curious about that which is
and that which strives to be.
Pushed by the bear's urgency, as if time is of the utmost,
with a hesitant heart, I step out onto a green common to
bright sunshine where I see a stone bench.
An exedra. A curved seat sheltered by stately pines
becomes my house of learning.
But there is no teacher.
Behind me Mukwoh growls approval,
giving me strength and courage to go forward.

My spirit breaks open, flows like a river released of ice.
I am set on a journey to discover language
and recognize who I am to be.

Glow

Why is it that apples glow
like a full moon
in an October sky?
White. Golden. Red.
Reminiscent too of
summer's august month
or the bite of frost on a
footprint significant in the
snow.

What is glow?
The gleam of a train light
on a track
seeking the way.
The shimmer of a dress
in all that glitz.

Where is glow?
In the passion of a poem
at midnight
writing the flame.

The line.

For Robert Frost

His voice was thick
as pine resin
when he began to read
and the words travelled
down my spine.

I saw a man picking apples
a man taking a road
different from mine,
a man who stopped to examine life
who took one step
above the earth to write
how he saw trees,
the mending of a wall,
a patch of snow,
and why boys liked birches.

He wrote the words
not because he wanted fame
but because he wanted the ordinary
to be significant
for the poem to be

the footprint
in the snow.

For Boris Pasternak

Green grows the morning:
the wind sighs across the short grass
sun stretching   glowing yellow on the rooftops.

The crow flies above,
his *aw* a croak
like an old man
clearing his throat—
or like the poet who hears such voices in his poem.

By afternoon
a grey-bearded sky hovers on the village
the silence so still
the acclaimed poet in his dacha puts down his pen.
Shadows are darkening the book he is writing.
His heart flutters.

                    Halts.

Under tall substantial pines
in a clearing beside a hill
they bury him
and the lone wolf
howls its lament into
the long wintery night.

When people ask
why did he fight the battle so long

tell them he fought for the pulse of the word.
The slant.

The Visit

I have a room full of poets
who sit on painted green shelves.
Sometimes in the
night when sleeps eludes me
they step from their slim volumes
in their rumpled sweaters.
Tonight Hardy, Eliot, Boland and Lorca arrive,
their melodious voices rising in the dark, their words
like shadows
on the wall.

Flames from a fire they rise
and spread, each spark
                    snapping into awareness
so quickly after the
other that I fear to breathe.

Eliot begins with *Let us go then, you and I...*
then Boland tells me about wolves and elms
and Hardy quiet in his corner with a gleam in his eyes
says:
Yes, trees even turning in their sleep…

The fire is hot and yet I thirst.
I want to snatch every word,
grasp their meaning.
My fingers burn
to light up the pages of my scribbler

and fill me with hope—
But wait.
They have all gone
slipping back into their books while I was busily engaged.

I hear Lorca singing softly, *A la nana, nana, nana.*

And the quiet creature I call hope
has gone to sleep as well.

Hope

is a stone, perhaps,
cerise or crimson
building one
colour upon the
other,

is a rose,
petals unfurled
and a bee at its
centre dancing
merrily,
sucking sweet nectar,

is the wind
that soughs
through
the evergreen
breathing in
and out.

In and out.

Bert Says, or, The First Time

We shall not cease from exploration
And the end of all our exploring
Will be to arrive where we started
And know the place for the first time.
– T. S. Eliot, Little Gidding

Bert says,
Seems these days we're at the end
of everything.
Dark suits ruling with words of gibble-gabble.
Don't amount to much. Call it glorification. Of sorts.
Maybe.
More like a weakness to make us poor.
How can we stop them?

Long time ago Mother Earth was
the strong one.
Pure. Majestic. Golden.
Then science became the master.
We waged a war.
Raped her. Gutted her.
Taking. Taking. Taking.
Oil, minerals and water.

That's not *our* way.

Wind says we know
about bees on flowers,

about silent deer
drinking at green pools,
their brown scamper into the woods.

Wind also says,
when we return to Mother Earth,
return to the spirits
remembering that we belong here,
when we hold aki in our hands,
feel her strength and give back to her bounty,
then we can emerge with hope.
With heart.

Like the first time.

Squall Variation

From the chair she reflects on days
when she played in the cold and allowed the wind
to paint her cheeks red,
to frost snow-mittened fingers
while the wind hurried snow down the street
                                        on long white gusts.

Now she sits, shoulders shawled,
feet in thick striped socks,
and watches the wind pluck snow
from the banks and fling it across
the frozen lowland.

She's starving for a hint of green.

February Afternoon

For months we've had cold
cars passing in the street,
wheels crunching on crisp snow.
After Christmas a stiff wind blew bitter air
down the bay and filled each pane of glass

with strange illustrations
sparkling white
as the sun shone bright.

Thoughts come of
grass growing green in the yard,
of another wind, a softer one,
that could dance Spring into being
that could bring blossoms to the cherry tree.
Shadows lengthen on the snow banks
and day fades to twilight.

There's a noise at the window:

Winter passes, laughing,
snow in his wake.

The Word

Snow fell
before the leaves,
surprised the still red rose,
filled the mean cracks
of pavement and
fixed mind's thoughts blue.

Came a whisper in the grass:

Winter.

Rain

The room grows dark and a strong wind outside
the dining-room window tosses the leaves
of the old oak towards the leaden sky.
The news is not good these days; society
too close, goodness lost to apathy.

Through the branches I see light in the sky
to the south and wonder how long I have
before the rain falls. I hurry outdoors,
unpin the clothes. Take each garment and sheet
in hand and begin to fold. Then the wind
blows in with a whoosh and I know soon
the drops will fall from the pewter sky
on my face and neck,
on the parched grass,
thirst yearning in each blade,
in a heart that seeks the tranquillity of rain.

Quest

When you died, I took the old and rusted scythe,
cut a swath through the grass, as if on a quest,
hacking at spider's webs, a wren's nest while
a snake slithered past the impending blade.
Whatever happened? -- What happens next? -- were my refrains
As I stood panting my heart sore my soul drained
I thought of how I miss your wit your smile your touch.
In horror I saw what I had done in my anguish
beheaded daisies bladderwort tall grasses.
Because with you forever gone
I felt I would never again know pleasure and so
I ravaged Mother Earth.
The things I harmed and cast away,
I now see their value.
Life will persevere.

Riddle

Why I dreamt of birds and bears
haunts me even now.
When the pale moon hung low
shining on those arctic winter nights,
images flickered and flowed.
Doves huddled in trees for warmth and
bears slept, their sleeping mouths tasting
the berries of summer.

The dream changed, blurred.

I became the dove that flew,
I became the bear that roared.
To this day their shapes hover
and I weigh
what those dreams may still give rise to.

Lumber

I dreamt I was piling words
the way my father stored softwood
layer upon layer
from pines: planks, long, straight and true.
I thought I could make a mark – the picking seemed
easy.

He cut hardwood as well, heaped the boards high.
I sought words in this vein, in
the density of oak I thought I needed
to add strength to the sentence,
piling words until they hemmed the sky,
but the sentence skidded,
                                        tumbled to one side.

I had loaded them one upon the other,
forgetting that
balance requires heart.

Lochranza Stones

The ferry is late. In a day of mist
and rain, cold enough to paint damp on bones,
I skip stones to pass morning's time,
gathering them from the shingle while deer
graze along the lush green shore
unafraid,
the stones dredged up from the hidden ocean floor,
altered by winds and storms:
feldspar, sandstone – bands of yellow
and red -- others I cannot name.

In One Moment

The white-haired woman
wiped her hands
on her printed blue apron
bent to retrieve the paper
someone had tossed
on the porch,
eyes meeting mine as
I drove past,
and turning,

she re-entered

her little

white house

and

shut the door.

A Fumble at the Stars

The river rumbles on, certain of its journey,
water tumbles over rocks
                                        pure and clear,
twigs caught in its grasp,
past childhood and dreams I hold so dear.

I seek new ways, fumble at the stars.
While moon's fingers played on the ceiling
I heard the siren call of the train whistle
and longed to leave the bush at first light.

Years pass. I reach my destination.
But amidst my efforts, the stars seem remote.
Cold. Then I consider the river, those past dreams.

Had I not ventured. Had I not been bold.

In a Room

full of shadows,
my father was waiting for the Old Ones.
He lay wrapped in sheets crisp and clean,
tightly tucked like cookies in a box.
I'd brought flowers that would soon droop and wilt,
watched his mouth aching for words.
I leaned forward and asked,
What is it, Dad?
What are you trying to say?
His voice rasped in the airless room
like the last dry leaf on a tree:

Heaven's a bit crowded right now.

Let's go to Tim's.

Assistant

Wind
shudders
at the edge
of the beach
weaves water
the shade of
an unripe apple
to the blue-grey morning
then whoops the raiment
over the wet sand
to the person
writing wildly
on the shore.

The Leaves of May

Did you know
that the loved ones now gone
are walking with the ancestors?
They are with the Creator who pauses
every now and then to see if you are
paying attention   to see if you are ready to
                    follow his ways.

If you are not, the
Creator will wait for you as
you smell the flower at the
bend in the road   or talk to the deer,
or pause and greet a neighbour,
lift the heart of a man
too blind to see.

And when you turn
at the entrance
of the forest
to see the sunlight scattered
across the leaves of May,
then it will be the time to walk
with the ancestors.

Acknowledgements

I want to thank Matt Joudrey of At Bay Press for having faith in my work and for this publication.

Also, many thanks to Jonina Kirton, my editor, for her keen eye in hunting out the errors, and for her conviction that I could go further. Thanks for those gentle and persistent nudges. Thanks, too, to my copy editor, Rachel Burlock, for her enthusiasm, for our chats and for the finishing touches required that I had little knowledge of.

Thanks to my friends and fellow writers who encouraged me on this journey into poetry.

Thanks, too, to Matthew Stevens and Matt Joudrey for their remarkable work on the book cover design. Fox turned out to be a fine fellow.

Thanks to my brother, Alf Dumont, who wanted to read my poems.

Miigwech to my brother, Jim Dumont, who sent me on a journey that led to the world of poetry.

Most of all, thanks to my husband, Bob, and to our children, Brenda, Tim and John who are always there.

Notes

"If You Stood on the Hill" is a variant of a line from John G. Neihardt's book *Black Elk Speaks: The Complete Edition,* University of Nebraska Press, 2014.

"she waits – a Penelope – watching." In Homer's *Odyssey,* Penelope is the wife of Odysseus who waits 20 years for his return after he fought in the Trojan Wars.

"guvment is a vernacular term for "government"; "white-bread" characterizes low paying jobs.

"Blue Sky Woman" was inspired by the work of Emily Dickinson.

"I Dreamed a Dream" is from *Les Miserables* first written by Alain Boublil and Jean-Marc Natel, Paris, 1980.

"Raider's March" was written by John Williams, London, Columbia Records, 1981.

The Mary Oliver quotation at the beginning of "What a Collection" is taken from "Ravens" in *New and Selected Poems: Volume Two,* Beacon Press Books, 2005.

"That Which Is and That Which Strives to Be" refers to the title of a painting by P. K. Page and is from *Journey with No Maps: A Life of P. K. Page* by Sandra Djwa, McGill's University Press, 2013. I was fascinated with the title and out of that a poem grew.

"For Robert Frost" was inspired after hearing the poet read a poem on *The Caedmon Poetry Collection: A Century of Poets Reading Their Work,* Harper Collins Publishers, 2000.

The word "trees" was inspired by Robert Frost's poem titled "The Sound of the Trees"; the line "a patch of snow" from the poet's poem "A Patch of Old Snow", and "why boys liked birches" inspired from the poem "Birches", all of these in *The Road Not Taken and Other Poems* by Robert Frost, Dover Publications, 2014. The phrase "a mending wall" was inspired from his poem "Mending Wall."

"For Boris Pasternak" was inspired from a reading of *The Zhivago Affair: The Kremlin, the CIA, and the Battle Over a Forbidden Book,* Peter Finn, 2013.

In Russia, a "dacha" is a cottage, used as a second or vacation home.

"Let us go then, you and I," is the opening line T. S. Eliot's poem, "The Love Song of J. Alfred Prufrock."

"wolves and elms" is a line from a poem by Eavan Boland titled "My Country in Darkness."

"Yes, trees even turning in their sleep…" is a line from a poem by Thomas Hardy titled "A Possession of Dead Days."

"A la nana, nana, nana" is a line from a cradle song that

Federico Garcia Lorca enjoyed very much.

The T. S. Eliot quotation at the beginning of 'Bert Says, or The First Time" is taken from "Little Gidding" of *Collected Poems 1909-1962,* Faber and Faber, 1963.

"A Fumble at the Stars" is a line from a poem by Louis MacNeice titled "Cradle Song for Eleanor."

Variations of the poems "In the Yellow Afternoon" and "Regeneration" appeared in *The Steel Chisel;* and "Woman Missing" in *Games Poets Play.*

"Inheritance" was inspired from reading Anne Michaels' poem titled "Lake of Two Rivers".

Ojibwe Glossary

There are many spellings of the following words depending on dialects and pronunciations. I have followed those outlined in the Anishinaubae Thesaurus by Basil H. Johnston, Michigan State University Press, 2007.

aundaeg	crow
Kitchi-Mukwoh	great bear
Geeziss	Father Sun
Kitchi-Manitou	Creator
waugoosh	fox
Cheeby-aub-oozoo	mystic musician
Mukwoh	bear
aki	land, earth

Of Ojibwe descent Mary Barnes is a graduate of the University of Waterloo and a winner of the Tom York Award for short fiction. She has written book reviews for The Antigonish Review and currently writes for Prairiefire. Her poetry has appeared in literary journals such as the Prairie Journal, Tower Poetry Society, and Voicings. Inspirations for her writing come from the landscape of her youth and everyday encounters. Born in Parry Sound, she now lives in Wasaga Beach with her husband Bob and writes, gardens and talks to the birds.